Fact Finders™

Questions and Answers: Physical Science

Magnetism

A Question and Answer Book

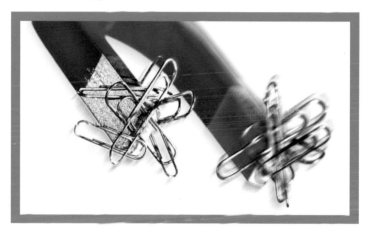

by Adele Richardson

Consultant:
Philip W. Hammer, PhD
Vice President, The Franklin Center
The Franklin Institute Science Museum
Philadelphia, Pennsylvania

Capstone
press
Mankato, Minnesota

Fact Finders is published by Capstone Press,
151 Good Counsel Drive, P.O. Box 669, Mankato, Minnesota 56002.
www.capstonepress.com

Library of Congress Cataloging-in-Publication Data
Richardson, Adele, 1966–
    Magnetism: a question and answer book / by Adele Richardson.
    p. cm—(Fact finders. Questions and answers. Physical science)
    Summary: "Introduces magnetism and the creation, forces, and applications of
magnets"—Provided by publisher.
    Includes bibliographical references and index.
    ISBN-13: 978-0-7368-5447-4 (hardcover)
    ISBN-10: 0-7368-5447-9 (hardcover)
    1. Magnetism—Juvenile literature. 2. Magnets—Juvenile literature. I. Title. II. Series.
QC753.7.R53 2006
538—dc22   2005020126

Editorial Credits
Chris Harbo, editor; Juliette Peters, designer; Tami Collins, illustrator; Jo Miller, photo
    researcher; Scott Thoms, photo editor

Photo Credits
AP/Wide World Photos/Ren Long, Xinhua, 10
Capstone Press/Gary Sundermeyer, 17, 27; Karon Dubke, 4, 8, 9, 11, 15, 18, 19, 21, 22,
    23, 29 (all)
Corbis/Tim Davis, 26
Getty Images Inc./Stone/Dennis Galante, 1
Grant Heilman Photography, 6
Photo Researchers, Inc./Science Photo Library/Cordelia Molloy, cover;
    Cristina Pedrazzinin, 16; Sheila Terry, 7; Simon Fraser, 25
Visuals Unlimited/Loren Winters, 14

1 2 3 4 5 6 11 10 09 08 07 06

Table of Contents

Features

What is magnetism?

It pushes. It pulls. It holds pictures to refrigerator doors. It's a force you can't see, but you use it every day. It's magnetism!

Did you know that the power of magnetism starts with **atoms**? Atoms are tiny particles that make up everything in the universe. In the center of an atom is a nucleus. Circling around the nucleus are tiny **electrons**. The way these electrons circle decides if something is magnetic or not.

Magnets turn a refrigerator door into a fun place to display pictures.

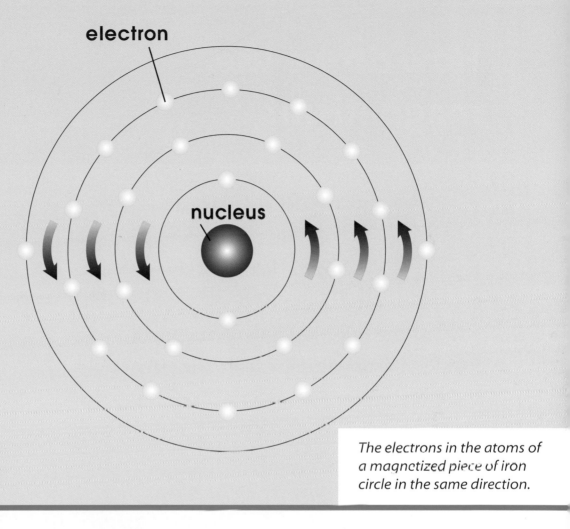

electron

nucleus

The electrons in the atoms of a magnetized piece of iron circle in the same direction.

Electrons in non-magnetic materials circle in many different directions. But when something is magnetic, most of its electrons circle in the same direction. The circling electrons create the magnetic force that **attracts** some metals toward a magnet.

5

How do we use magnetism?

Every day, we use magnets and magnetism in countless ways. Some cabinet doors have magnetic latches to help them stay shut. A refrigerator door does too. The edge of the door has a long, magnetic strip inside the rubber door seal. The strip sticks to the metal refrigerator so the door stays shut.

hard disk

*A computer hard disk is coated
with magnetic material that
helps the disk store information.*

But magnets do more than just hold
doors shut. Magnets inside computers store
information. Credit cards have thin magnetic
strips that store names and account numbers.
And do you like to listen to music? Guess
what? Your stereo speakers use magnets to
change electric signals into sound.

Why doesn't a penny stick to a magnet?

Actually, it depends on what the penny is made of. A U.S. penny is made of zinc and copper. Neither of these metals are magnetic. No matter how hard you try, a magnet won't pick up a U.S. penny.

A magnet's power doesn't affect a pile of U.S. pennies.

British pennies have enough steel in them to stick to a magnet.

Metals such as iron, steel, cobalt, and nickel are magnetic. They can be pulled toward a magnet. British pennies have a layer of copper on the outside. But their insides are steel. So a magnet can pick up British pennies.

Why don't some magnets stick together?

Have you ever tried putting two magnets together? Sometimes magnets feel like they are pushing away from each other. They are.

The ends of a magnet have **poles**. One end is the north pole, and the other is the south pole. The way two magnets act with each other depends on these poles.

Fact!

Maglev trains don't touch their tracks! They use the pushing power of magnetism to float over the tracks and to move forward and backward.

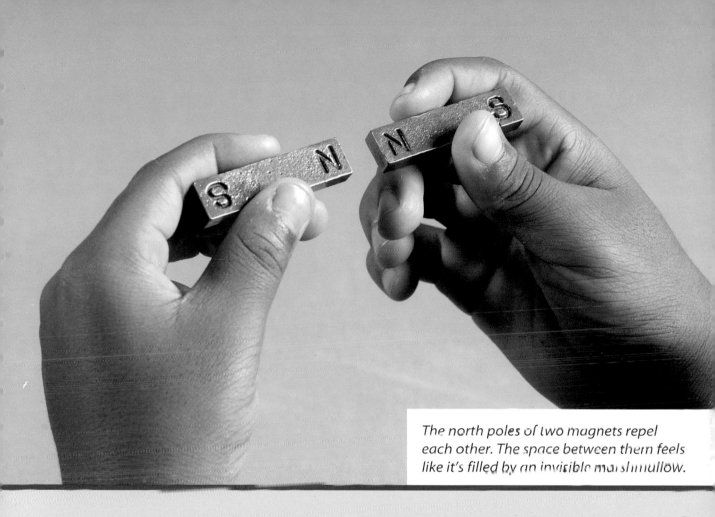

The north poles of two magnets repel each other. The space between them feels like it's filled by an invisible marshmallow.

For magnets, the rules are "likes **repel**" and "opposites attract." The same poles of two magnets always push each other away. To get the magnets to attract each other just turn one of the magnets around. When the north pole and the south pole meet, the magnets stick together.

If the earth has two poles, is it a magnet?

Yes, it is! Earth is a magnet. But not because it has a North Pole and a South Pole. Scientists believe earth's magnetism is created deep underground. They think that as the planet spins, melted iron swirling around earth's core creates magnetism.

Fact!

Did you know earth's magnetic poles are always moving? The poles move about 25 miles (40 kilometers) each year.

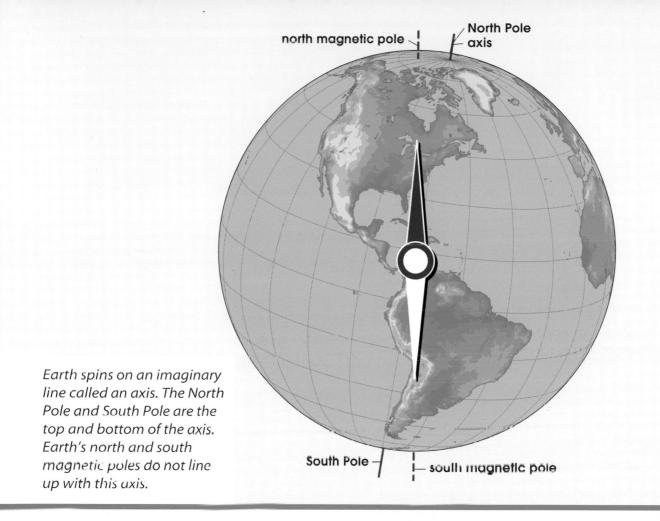

north magnetic pole

North Pole
axis

Earth spins on an imaginary line called an axis. The North Pole and South Pole are the top and bottom of the axis. Earth's north and south magnetic poles do not line up with this axis.

South Pole

south magnetic pole

Just like any other magnet, earth has magnetic poles. But these poles are separate from the North and South Poles. Earth's magnetic poles are a few hundred miles (kilometers) away from the North and South Poles. In fact, earth's north magnetic pole is near Canada.

What is a magnetic field?

A magnet's power is strongest at its poles. But the rest of the magnet has power too. A magnetic field is the area around a magnet that attracts or repels magnetic metals. The magnetic field's size depends on the strength of the magnet. A weak magnet has a smaller magnetic field than a strong magnet. Either way, an object must be inside the magnetic field to be pulled toward or pushed away from the magnet.

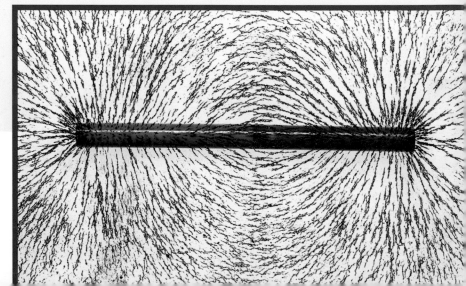

Iron filings form lines around a magnet. These lines show how far the magnetic field extends beyond the magnet.

A magnetic glass cleaner clamps onto the outside and inside of an aquarium. Its magnetic power is strong enough to work through glass and water.

Magnetic fields can reach through some materials to attract or repel objects. As long as the magnets are strong enough, they work through things such as cardboard, aluminum foil, cloth, and paper. Magnets can even attract or repel objects underwater.

How does a compass work?

People use compasses to tell what direction they are moving in. The needle of a compass is a magnet. Because it spins freely, it turns toward earth's magnetic poles. The south pole of the needle is marked with a color, such as red or yellow. This end always points to earth's magnetic north pole. No matter which direction you turn, the needle always points north.

The yellow end of the compass needle is drawn toward earth's north magnetic pole.

A compass is great for finding north. But you can use it to help you find east, west, and south too.

How do you find other directions with a compass? It's easier than you might think. To find west, hold the compass level. Then, turn the compass so the letter W is on top. Now, slowly turn your body until the tip of the needle points to the letter N. When it does, you are facing west.

Why does a line of paper clips hang off a magnet?

Magnets can pass their magnetism to some other objects. A paper clip stuck to a magnet becomes a **temporary** magnet itself. As long as it touches the magnet, the paper clip can attract another paper clip. Likewise, the second paper clip, now touching the first one, will also become magnetic. See how long you can make a paper clip chain.

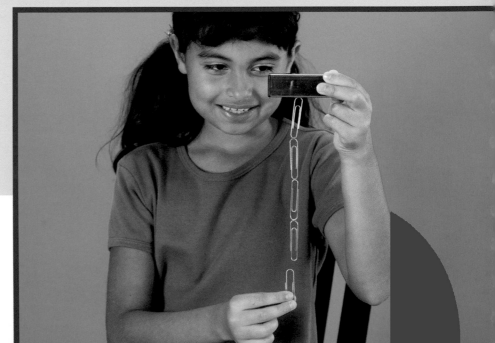

How long can it get? Strong magnets can turn paper clips into temporary magnets.

When the first paper clip is removed from the magnet, all of the paper clips lose their magnetism.

Why can't your paper clip chain go on forever? Because the paper clips near the end of the chain have a weaker power of magnetism than those closer to the magnet. And what happens if you take the first paper clip off the magnet? All of the paper clips lose their magnetic power. The chain falls apart.

Do magnets last forever?

Magnets don't last forever. But they will last for many years if they are not dropped or heated. Why? Because the atoms in a magnet line up in magnetic **domains**. All of the domains in a magnet point in the same direction. As long as the domains stay that way, the magnet has its power.

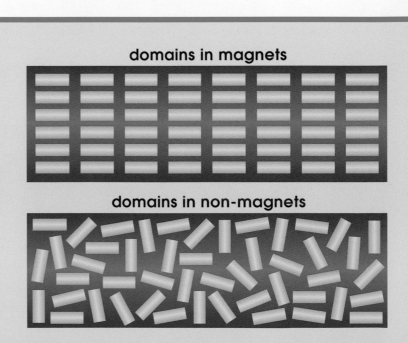

domains in magnets

domains in non-magnets

The domains of a magnet are lined up in rows. The domains in non-magnets are disorganized.

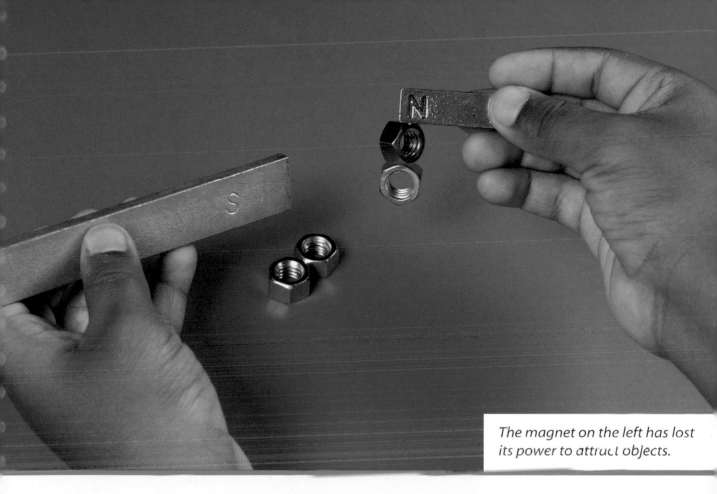

The magnet on the left has lost its power to attract objects.

A magnet loses its power when its domains start pointing in different directions. Dropping or hitting a magnet makes some domains change the way they point. Heating a magnet will cause its domains to change direction, too. When enough domains change direction, the magnet loses its power.

How are magnets made?

Some magnets are found in nature. **Magnetite**, also known as lodestone, is the most magnetic rock on earth. Magnetite is made of iron. When magnetite formed, the domains in the iron were drawn toward earth's magnetic poles. The domains point in the same direction, so magnetite is magnetic.

Fact!

Sometimes the black sand grains you see on a sandy beach are tiny grains of magnetite. You can tell for sure if they stick to a magnet.

Rubbing a nail in one direction on a magnet will give the nail the power of magnetism.

People can make magnets too. Most magnets are made with iron or steel. A nail can be **magnetized** by rubbing it on a magnet in one direction for a long time. The magnet causes the domains in the metal to point in the same direction. Once magnetized, they will pull other magnetic metals toward them.

What are electromagnets?

Electromagnets use electricity to create their power of magnetism. Electricity moving along a straight wire creates a magnetic field. This magnetic field gets weaker as it moves away from the wire. But if the wire is coiled, the magnetic field is forced back toward the wire and it becomes stronger. Electromagnets are made of coils of wire called **solenoids**.

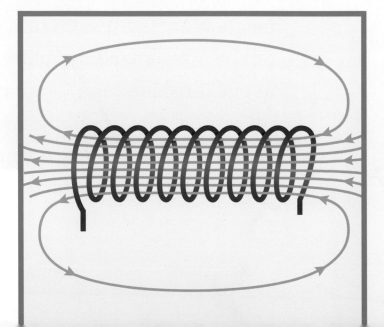

The blue lines represent the magnetic field created by a solenoid.

A crane uses a huge electromagnet to pick up scrap metal at a junkyard.

Electromagnets are useful because they turn on and off. When electricity flows through the coiled wire, the magnet works. When the power is cut, the electromagnet drops whatever it was holding. Huge electromagnets are great tools in junkyards. An electromagnet on a crane can pick up scrap metal. Then, with a flick of a switch the electromagnet can be shut off. No more magnetism. The metal falls into a pile.

How long have people used magnetism?

The ancient Greeks gave magnetism its name at least 2,000 years ago. When they found magnetite, they discovered it had the power to attract iron. The Greeks named the power magnetism after the Magnetes. The Magnetes were the people who lived in Magnesia where the lodestone was found.

Fact!

Some animals, like birds, can sense earth's magnetic field. It helps them find their way while migrating.

Early Chinese people are known to have made compasses with magnetite. They floated a thin piece of magnetite on a cork in a bowl of water. Just like compasses today, the magnetite always pointed toward earth's magnetic poles. These early compasses helped people find direction.

Fast Facts about Magnetism

- A magnet always has north and south poles. Cutting a magnet in half makes two magnets, each with two poles.

- Magnetism is created when most of an atom's electrons circle in the same direction.

- Earth's magnetic field reaches about 37,000 miles (59,540 kilometers) into space.

- The ends of a compass needle always point toward earth's north and south magnetic poles.

- Some magnets are found naturally in the earth. Others can be made from magnetic materials.

- Iron, steel, cobalt, and nickel are common magnetic metals.

- Magnets can lose their magnetism if they are dropped, hit, or heated.

- An electromagnet uses electricity to create a strong magnetic field in a coil of wire.

Hands On: Make an Electromagnet

Electromagnets seem complicated, but they're actually fairly easy to make. Ask an adult to help you with this activity to make your own electromagnet.

What You Need

copper wire, 12 inches (30 centimeters) long
iron nail
D-size battery
paper clips

What You Do

1. *Tightly wrap the copper wire around the nail 10 to 15 times. Leave about 3 inches (8 centimeters) of wire unwrapped at each end of the nail.*
2. *Press one end of the wire to the positive end of the battery with your thumb. Press the other end of the wire to the negative end of the battery with your index finger.*
3. *Holding the battery and wires together, pass the nail and coiled wire over the paper clips. Watch what happens.*

Why did the nail and coiled wire pick up the paper clips? Because the electricity from the battery created a magnetic field in the coiled wire. What happens if you pick up some paper clips and then let go of one of the wires on the battery? What happens if you put more or less coils in your wire? Try these experiments with your new electromagnet.

Glossary

atom (AT-uhm)—an element in its smallest form

attract (uh-TRAKT)—to pull together; a magnet attracts iron.

domain (doh-MAYN)—a group of magnetic atoms

electron (i-LEK-tron)—a tiny particle in an atom that travels around the nucleus

magnetite (MAG-nuh-tite)—a hard, black rock found in the earth that attracts iron; magnetite is also known as lodestone.

magnetize (MAG-nuh-tize)—to make a piece of material magnetic

pole (POHL)—one of the two ends of a magnet; a pole can also be the top or bottom part of a planet.

repel (ri-PEL)—to push apart; like poles of magnets repel each other.

solenoid (SOH-luh-noid)—a coil of wire that makes a magnetic field when electricity moves through it

temporary (TEM-puh-rer-ee)—lasting only a short time

Internet Sites

FactHound offers a safe, fun way to find Internet sites related to this book. All of the sites on FactHound have been researched by our staff.

Here's how:
1. Visit *www.facthound.com*
2. Type in this special code **0736854479** for age-appropriate sites. Or enter a search word related to this book for a more general search.
3. Click on the **Fetch It** button.

FactHound will fetch the best sites for you!

Read More

Cooper, Christopher. *Magnetism: From Pole to Pole.* Science Answers. Chicago: Heinemann, 2004.

Morgan, Ben. *Magnetism.* Elementary Physics. San Diego: Blackbirch Press, 2003.

Stille, Darlene R. *Magnetism.* Science Around Us. Chanhassen, Minn.: Child's World, 2005.

Tiner, John Hudson. *Magnetism.* Understanding Science. Mankato: Smart Apple Media, 2003.

Index